Health and My Body

Flu

Beth Bence Reinke

raintree
a Capstone company — publishers for children

Raintree is an imprint of Capstone Global Library Limited, a company incorporated in England and Wales having its registered office at 264 Banbury Road, Oxford, OX2 7DY – Registered company number: 6695582

www.raintree.co.uk
myorders@raintree.co.uk

Hardback edition text © Capstone Global Library Limited 2022
Paperback edition text © Capstone Global Library Limited 2023
The moral rights of the proprietor have been asserted.

All rights reserved. No part of this publication may be reproduced in any form or by any means (including photocopying or storing it in any medium by electronic means and whether or not transiently or incidentally to some other use of this publication) without the written permission of the copyright owner, except in accordance with the provisions of the Copyright, Designs and Patents Act 1988 or under the terms of a licence issued by the Copyright Licensing Agency, 5th Floor, Shackleton House, 4 Battle Bridge Lane, London SE1 2HX (www.cla.co.uk). Applications for the copyright owner's written permission should be addressed to the publisher.

Edited by Gena Chester
Designed by Kazuko Collins
Original illustrations © Capstone Global Library Limited 2022
Picture research by Jo Miller
Production by Tori Abraham
Originated by Capstone Global Library Ltd

978 1 3982 2516 9 (hardback)
978 1 3982 2515 2 (paperback)

British Library Cataloguing in Publication Data
A full catalogue record for this book is available from the British Library.

Acknowledgements
We would like to thank the following for permission to reproduce photographs:
Alamy: ZUMA Press Inc, 17; iStockphoto: PaulGregg, 9; Science Source: Hazel Appleton, Health Protection Agency Centre for Infections, 7; Shutterstock: cabania, 21, Daisy Daisy, 25, DG PhotoStock, 23, Inside Creative House, 29, Irina Borsuchenko, 19, Krakenimages.com, 27, Motortion Films, 11, New Africa, 15, pavla, 5, photonova, design element, Primeiya, Cover, Prostock-studio, 13.

Every effort has been made to contact copyright holders of material reproduced in this book. Any omissions will be rectified in subsequent printings if notice is given to the publisher.

All the internet addresses (URLs) given in this book were valid at the time of going to press. However, due to the dynamic nature of the internet, some addresses may have changed, or sites may have changed or ceased to exist since publication. While the author and publisher regret any inconvenience this may cause readers, no responsibility for any such changes can be accepted by either the author or the publisher.

Contents

What is flu? 4

How the flu spreads 8

Your body and the flu 12

Treating the flu 16

Preventing the flu 22

Staying well 26

    Glossary 30

    Find out more 31

    Index 32

Words in **bold** are in the glossary.

What is flu?

Flu is short for influenza. Influenza is an infection of the body's **airways**. It's caused by a tiny germ called a **virus**. The influenza virus attacks the nose and throat. It often infects the lungs too.

There are three main types of flu viruses. They are types A, B and C.

The flu virus attacks the body's airways.

Types A and B can cause severe illness. There are many kinds of type A flu viruses. Type A can infect humans and some animals. Horses, pigs and birds can get type A flu. Types B and C flu viruses only infect people. Type C only causes mild **symptoms**.

New flu viruses often develop. Sometimes they cause **pandemics**. A pandemic is a period of time when an illness spreads to people all around the world. In 1918, there was a flu pandemic. The most recent flu pandemic was in 2009.

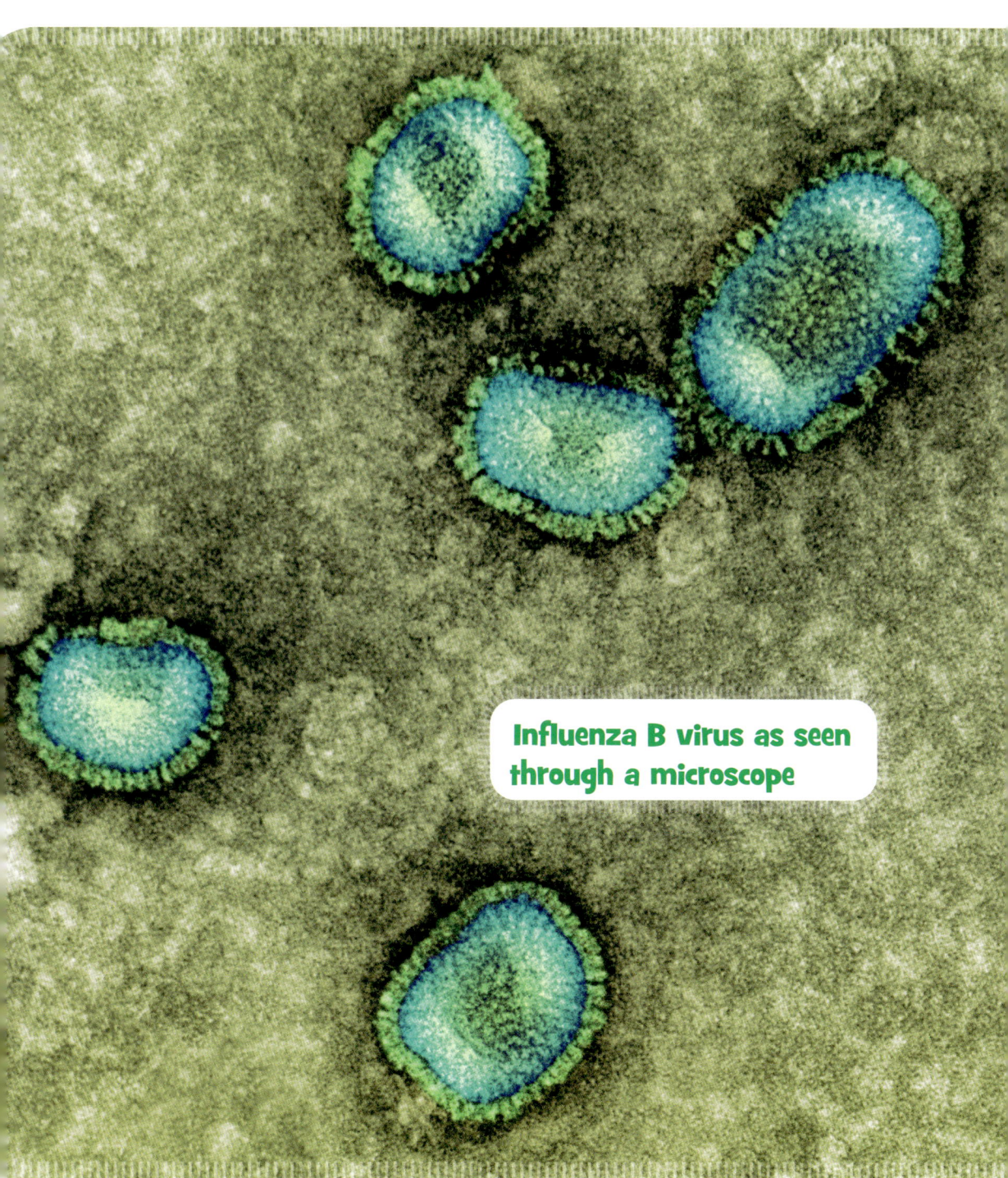
Influenza B virus as seen through a microscope

How the flu spreads

The flu is **contagious**. It spreads from person to person. Millions of people become ill during flu season. It lasts from late autumn to spring. But most people get the flu in winter.

Influenza viruses spread in tiny droplets. The droplets spread in two ways. They move through the air. They also land on objects.

You sneeze into the air. Achoo! Droplets spray from your nose. They fly out of your mouth when you cough too.

The droplets can land on other people. The virus gets in their noses, eyes or mouths. Then they might get ill with the flu.

Droplets can land on things. Flu viruses can stay on these things for about two days. Other people touch the objects. They get the virus on their hands. Then they rub their eyes. Or they touch their nose or mouth.

Then the flu virus gets into their body. It takes over cells in the airways. The cells make many more viruses. About two days later, the person has symptoms of the flu.

Your body and the flu

Anyone can get the flu. Babies can become very ill. Pregnant women can too. Adults over 65 can have severe flu symptoms. So can people with heart or lung problems.

Flu symptoms come on quickly. You usually get a high fever with the flu. You may shiver from chills. Your whole body aches, even your head. You get a cough and sore throat. Your nose may be stuffy. And you feel very tired.

There are many symptoms of the flu.

Children can have extra flu symptoms. They might vomit. They may have diarrhoea. But adults don't often get those symptoms.

The flu lasts about a week. But some symptoms can stay with you. Your cough may last longer. You may feel tired for almost a month.

The flu can also cause other infections. Some people get ear infections. Others get a serious infection in their lungs called pneumonia.

Treating the flu

Doctors can usually tell if you have the flu. They know because of your symptoms. But sometimes they do a flu test to make sure.

A nurse swabs your nose. The swab gathers **mucus**. Scientists test the mucus. The test shows if you have the flu. Results may be ready in a few hours.

A medical professional can give someone a flu test.

If you have the flu, take care of yourself. Get plenty of sleep. Resting helps your body fight the virus.

Fluids help keep your body strong. Drink a lot of water. You can drink hot tea or soup. Hot drinks help loosen mucus. They unclog your nose. Cold drinks soothe your throat. Try a smoothie or ice lolly.

Humid air helps you breathe easier. Use a warm mist **humidifier**. Or breathe in steam from a bowl of hot water.

Drinking hot tea helps to ease flu symptoms.

Medicine

Medicine doesn't make the flu go away. But it helps you feel better. Some medicines lower your fever. They can ease your body aches too. Other kinds help your cough. A trusted adult can give you medicine.

A doctor may give you **antiviral** medicine. It works best in the first two days of the flu. This medicine does not cure the flu. But it helps you get better faster.

Medicine can help people feel better, but it cannot cure the flu.

Preventing the flu

The flu spreads easily. But you can help stop the spread. If you are ill, stay at home.

Don't share food or drinks. Cover your sneezes and coughs. Cough into your elbow. Keep tissues nearby. Sneeze into them. Wash your hands after.

Hot water destroys the flu virus. So do cleaning products. A trusted adult can help you clean things. They can wipe down things you touched. They can wash your towels and sheets.

Wash your hands often. Washing gets rid of the flu virus. Use warm water and soap. Rub your palms together. Wash the tops of your hands. Scrub between your fingers. Get your fingernails clean too.

It takes 20 seconds to get your hands clean. Singing a song helps you wash long enough. Sing the "Happy Birthday" song twice. Hum the alphabet. Try counting to 20 slowly.

Staying well

Staying healthy can help fight the flu virus. You can help your body stay well. Follow these tips:

Get plenty of sleep. Children need about 10 hours each night. Your body heals during sleep.

Eat healthy foods. Fruit and vegetables help keep you well. Eat some of each every day.

Exercise each day. Moving your body makes it strong.

Try not to worry. Stress is bad for your health.

Eating vegetables helps keep you healthy.

Vaccines

The flu **vaccine** helps prevent influenza. It's a liquid that contains parts of flu viruses. The flu vaccine is safe for most people over 6 months old.

Scientists create a new flu vaccine every year. That's because flu viruses change. It's important to get a flu vaccine every year.

The vaccine is given in an injection. It goes in your arm. The vaccine can also be in a spray. It goes in your nose. Your doctor knows which type is best for you.

It takes two weeks for the vaccine to work. It helps your body make **antibodies**. Antibodies fight the flu virus. They are an important step in staying healthy.

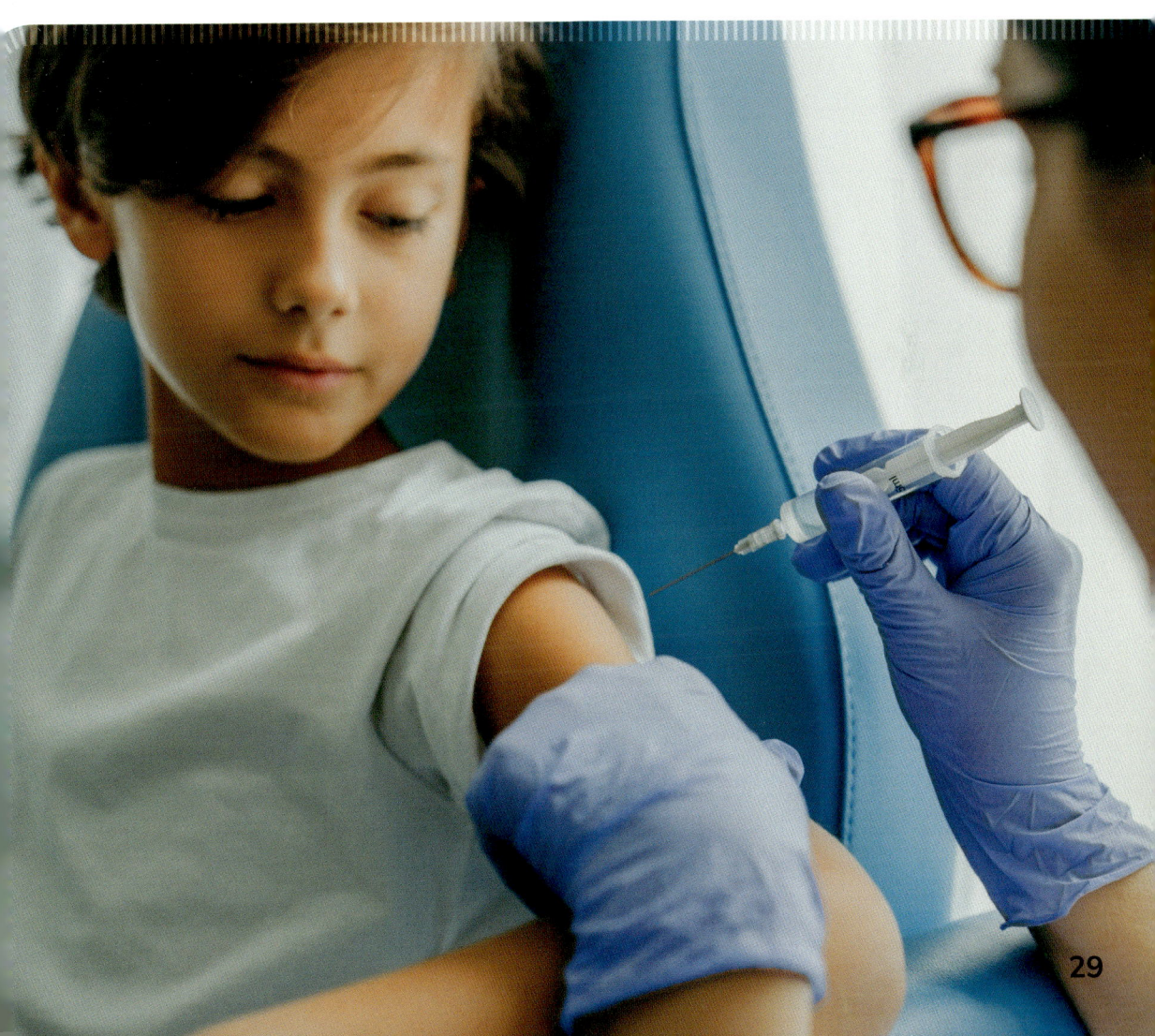

Glossary

airway breathing passage such as the nose, throat and lungs

antibody substance in the body that fights against infection and disease

antiviral describes a drug that fights a virus

contagious easy to spread

humidifier device used to create and keep damp air in a room

mucus liquid made by cells inside the nose and breathing passages

pandemic disease outbreak that spreads across the world

symptom sign the body shows when you are ill

vaccine substance that helps the body protect itself from a specific germ

virus tiny germ that can make people ill

Find out more

Books

History Smashers: Plagues and Pandemics, Kate Messner (Random House, 2021)

Pandemic Planet: How Diseases Impact Our World, Anna Claybourne (Franklin Watts, 2022)

The Deadliest Diseases Then and Now, Deborah Hopkinson (Scholastic Focus, 2021)

Website

www.healthforkids.co.uk/staying-healthy/stopping-flu/
This website tells you how to avoid spreading the flu to others.

Index

airways 4, 10
animals 6
antibodies 29

cleaning 22
contagious 8
cures 20

doctors 16, 20, 28
droplets 8, 10

exercising 27
eyes 10

fluids 18
flu seasons 8
foods 26

hands 10
humidifiers 18

infections 4, 14

lungs 4

medicines 20
mouths 10
mucus 16

noses 4, 8, 10, 12, 16, 18, 28
nurses 16

pandemics 6

resting 18, 26

scientists 16, 28
sharing 22
spreading 22
stress 27
symptoms 6, 10, 12, 14, 16, 20

tests 16
throats 4, 12, 18
types 4, 6

vaccines 28–29
viruses 4, 6, 8, 10, 22, 26, 28–29

washing 22, 24